Dropping Our Nets: Walking in His Footsteps

Bert Spann
Paul Gillespie
Mark Whitehead

FIRST EDITION

First Printing: 2017

ISBN 978-1-365-71359-0

For more resources to use in conjunction with this study (including videos and a companion teaching guide), visit www.corbanresourceoutfitters.org.

TABLE OF CONTENTS

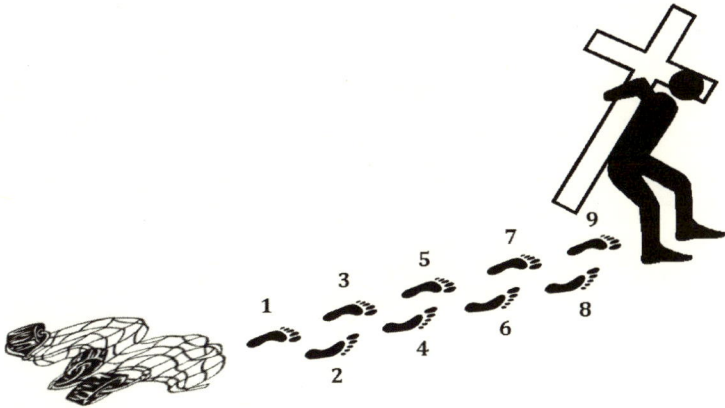

ACKNOWLEDGEMENTS

We are especially grateful to the following people for allowing us to use portions of their published material in *Dropping Our Nets: Walking in His Footsteps*.

Kenson Kuba for graciously allowing us to use his discipleship material. (www.discipleshipministry.com).

Dr. Gary Hill for giving us permission to use terms and definitions from *The Discovery Bible*. (www.thediscoverybible.com).

Herb Hodges, for allowing us to use terms and definitions from his book, *Tally Ho the Fox*. (www.herbhodges.com).

Scott Duvall and Danny Hays for allowing us to use portions from *Grasping God's Word*.

DROPPING OUR NETS: WALKING IN HIS FOOTSTEPS

INTRODUCTION

Matthew 4:18-20 tells us that as Jesus was walking along the Sea of Galilee, He saw two fishermen casting their nets into the lake. They were Simon (also called Peter) and his brother, Andrew. Jesus asked them to come and follow Him and He would make them fishers of men. They immediately dropped their nets and followed Jesus.

From the time Jesus first had followers, they had a choice to make. Were they going to hold on to their old life or were they going to follow Him? These two men were fishermen and they dropped their nets and left them to follow Jesus.

This study is titled *Dropping Our Nets* because just as these two men left their nets and their old life to follow Jesus, every believer must also turn from their old life and follow after Him. Your decision to follow Jesus is the most important decision in your life. Since you have decided to follow Him, you have a new life. It is up to you to drop your old life and follow in His footsteps.

Just like you had to learn to walk when you were a small child, you must now learn to walk as Jesus walked. Learning to walk as a child happens one step at a time and that is also how you will learn to follow Jesus. It is a process that begins with that first step and will continue one step at a time for the rest of your life. This study lays out nine basic steps to help you begin to follow Jesus.

THE BIBLE IS GOD'S WORD

You must understand that the Bible is God's word and as written in its original language, it is without error. It was written by people who were inspired by God. Look at a Bible's Table of Contents and you will see 66 individual books listed and they are divided into an Old Testament and a New Testament. The Old Testament contains 39 books and begins with God's creation of the universe and His creation of mankind. It is basically the story of God's people and the nation of Israel. The New Testament has 27 books. It begins with four biographical writings of Jesus and these four books are called "the Gospels." Most of the remainder of the New Testament is the story of the beginning and growth of the Christian Church .

There are many different translations of the Bible; but you need to select a version that is easy to read and understand. Your teacher can help you in this selection.

A good place to start reading is in the Gospel of John. Find the book of John in your Bible's Table of Contents and note that John is in the New Testament. Now locate the book of John. Notice how it is divided into chapters and chapters are divided into numbered verses so that they are easier to locate and reference. Go to chapter 3, then go to verse 16. You have found John 3:16 which you have probably heard before. Every book is laid out this way. Each book in the Bible contains at least one chapter and several verses. The Bible can be somewhat intimidating to a new believer but you will learn more about the Bible during this study.

THIS STUDY

This material will provide you with basic information about what it means to be a believer and follower of Jesus Christ and will also introduce you to how to study the Bible. Each lesson in this book is called a "footstep" because you must walk in His footsteps as you follow Him. There are a total of nine footsteps and each one is listed in the Table of Contents in this book. Each lesson will begin with an introduction, introduce several points to learn, and suggest one or more Bible verses to memorize. Some of the lessons may also include a section that lists some things for further exploration and identify additional resources for further study. Internet addresses, DVD's and books identified in this material are offered only as suggested resources

Because nearly 800 million people in the world cannot read or may have no written language, images are included in this book to assist in understanding its content. Each lesson contains images to provide additional information or identify actions for you to take. For example:

This image tells you there is a question for you to answer.

This image shows you to memorize a Bible verse.

This symbol requests you to read one or more Bible verses.

This symbol asks you to underline or circle specific words in your Bible.

This symbol tells you the word is defined in the glossary.

In addition, images are used to represent important points that you need to remember. These images should help you recall these points simply by remembering the image and will be helpful if you teach this to someone who does not read very well.

2

In this book you will see numerous references to Bible verses, but the Bible text is not included. This was done because you need to become familiar with your Bible and learn how to locate its books and verses. Do not be self-conscious about using the Bible Table of Contents to locate a Bible book.

As you go through this study, please keep some paper and a pencil or pen handy so you can take notes and also make notes in your Bible. Your notes will be helpful to you as you continue to learn how to follow Jesus. There are also several words used in this book that you are probably not familiar with and these words and their definitions are included in a glossary at the end of his book.

BEFORE YOU BEGIN THIS STUDY

- ✓ Be sure to have a pencil or pen and some paper available to take notes.
- ✓ Have access to a Bible.
- ✓ Watch the HOPE video online at www.thehopeproject.com.

You are also encouraged to complete the information below for your own personal use.

Name of person who shared Christ with me	
Street Address	
City/State/ZIP	
Telephone Number	
Email Address	

"God never takes away something from your life without replacing it with something better"

-Billy Graham

FOOTSTEP 1
SAFETY WHEN I LET GO

INTRODUCTION

If you died today, how sure are you that you have eternal life? Put a mark on the line below that best reflects your answer.

DO YOU HAVE ETERNAL LIFE??

NOT SURE	MAYBE	ABSOLUTELY SURE

There are many people who have attended church for years who are still not absolutely certain. Being sure you have eternal life involves being certain of your **decision** to trust in Jesus Christ as Savior! The following explains this important decision.

1. GOD, OUR CREATOR, LOVES US!

Read John 3:16
- *Circle* the **word** that describes God's **attitude** toward us.
- *Underline* the **phrase** that explains **how** God demonstrated His Love.
- *Circle* what we must **do** to obtain **Eternal life**.
- *Underline* to **whom** Eternal life is offered to.

   According to John 3:16, does God love you?
   ☐ **Yes** ☐ **No**

God's Love

Love is translated from a word (Agape), which in the original language means, "that which describes a love that is spiritual more than emotional." Whereas emotional love is often self-centered, "Agape" love values the thing loved, and seeks its best no matter the cost to the one loving it.

Read John 10:10
- *Underline* **why** Jesus said He came.
- *Circle* what **kind** of life He wants us to have.

   Would you like to have this kind of life?
   ☐ **Yes** ☐ **No**

2. OUR SIN HAS SEPARATED US FROM GOD

Read Romans 3:23
- *Circle* how **many** people have sinned.

Read Romans 6:23
- *Underline* the **result** of sin.

Spiritual death

The penalty for our sin is death. This death is more than just our bodies dying; it is spiritual separation from God. At our physical death, this separation becomes eternal. The separation between sinful man and God is so vast that no matter how "good" we may be, we are powerless to bridge it. Doing so would be like trying to reach the moon by jumping. No matter how high a person can jump, it is impossible.

3. JESUS CHRIST, GOD'S SON, DIED ON THE CROSS FOR OUR SINS

Read John 14:6
- *Circle* **three things** Jesus claims for Himself.
- *Underline* **who** is able to come to God **apart** from Christ.

    What does Jesus mean when He claims to be the Way? The Truth? The Life?

Read Romans 5:8
- *Underline* **how** God has demonstrated His love for us.
- *Circle* what **condition** we were in when God loved us.

Read 1 Corinthians 15:3-8
- *Underline* **four things** Christ did.
- *Circle* **all** the people to whom Christ appeared **alive** after rising from the dead.

    Do you think all of these people could have been mistaken? Why or Why not?

4.   WE ARE SAVED BY THE CROSS!

Read 1 John 2:1-2

- *Underline **three descriptions** of Christ.*

- What is propitiation (or atoning sacrifice)?

Read 1 Peter 2:24

- *Circle what he **bore** for us.*
- *Underline **how** we are healed.*

5.   WE ARE SAVED INTO THE CROSS

Read Romans 1:1

- *Underline the **first** descriptive word Paul uses to **describe himself** as a new believer?*

- What is a **bond-servant**?

Read Matthew 16:24

- *Underline the three **actions** you must take as a believer.*

- Is **take up your cross** an active or passive word?

Read 1 John 2:6

- If we say Jesus has saved us, *underline* the **phrase** that describes **how** we are to conduct our lives.

Read 1 Peter 4:12-19

- *Circle the **repeated words** in these verses that relate to experiencing something unpleasant.*

Reflection question: What does it look like to **suffer** for Jesus?

6. ASSURANCE OF ETERNAL LIFE

Read 1 John 5:11-13 and answer the questions below to learn how you can be certain you have eternal life in Jesus Christ.

- *Circle* what God has ***given*** to us.
- *Underline **where*** eternal life is found.
- *Circle* what a person ***has*** if he has Jesus Christ.
- *Underline* what a person does ***not*** have if he does not have Jesus Christ.

According to this passage, can a person ***know for sure*** he has eternal life?

☐ **Yes** ☐ **No**

- *Circle* this passage's ***answer*** to this question.
- *Underline **who can know*** they have eternal life.

Do you have Christ in your life?

☐ **Yes** ☐ **No**

If "***yes***," what else did you receive from God?

☐ *A perfect face and body to match.*
☐ *Financial riches.*
☐ *Eternal life.*

7. BASIS FOR OUR ASSURANCE

Eternal life is not based on how good we are, or how we feel. It is based on our **faith** in **Jesus Christ**. Notice that the teaching in 1 John 5:11-13 is written to those who **believe** in the Name of the Son of God!

Read Romans 1:16-17

- *Underline* to whom ***salvation*** is given.
- *Circle **what*** the righteous person should live by.

NOW WHAT?

We will close with the same question with which we began.

If you died today, are you **sure** you have eternal life?

☐ **Yes** ☐ **No**

Memorize *Romans 6:23*

Affirmation 1. Christ died on the cross for me. 2. God will receive me in heaven when I die because He promised He would. 3. I have eternal life because I have Christ.	We need to understand that **ETERNAL LIFE** is **NOW**; now just when we die! **A Prayer** Father, I praise You, for You have promised eternal life to all who believe in your Son Jesus Christ and Your promises are sure, for You cannot lie, nor do You change Your mind. You are faithful in all Your ways, and I thank you for the assurance I have in Christ. Amen.

RECOMMENDED RESOURCE

Book: *The Case for Christ: A Journalist's Personal Investigation of the Evidence for Jesus* by Lee Strobel

"Sin will take you farther than you want to go, keep you longer than you want to stay, and cost you more than you want to pay."

-Author Unknown

FOOTSTEP 2
DROPPING MY OLD LIFE

INTRODUCTION

How would you complete the following statement? When a person becomes a Christian,

☐ only those sins that he confesses are forgiven.
☐ all of his sins in the past are forgiven, but not those in the future.
☐ he becomes perfect and unable to ever sin again.
☐ all of our sins past, present & future are forgiven.

A problem facing all Christians is **sin**. In this lesson, we will not only learn the correct answer to the above statement, but also God's solution to help Christians overcome sin in their lives!

COMMON QUESTIONS ABOUT SIN:

1. WHAT IS SIN?

The word **sin** in the original language means "missing the mark" or "to do wrong." It describes the distance between where an arrow lands and the bull's eye of the intended target. Notice how it is used in the following Bible passages:

Read Romans 3:23
   Underline what **sin** is.

> **Sin** is *falling short of the glory of God*. Sin is *Man's failure* to live up to the *perfect standard* of God. We have all broken God's perfect moral law, either in action or in thought. Even our failure to do what we know is right is sin. So there is no one innocent or perfect among us.

Read James 2:10
   Circle the words that **describe us** if we only break one point of the law.

Read James 4:17
It is also sin if we know the right thing to do but we do **not** do it.

☐ TRUE ☐ FALSE

11

2. WHAT ARE THE COMMON TRAPS FOR SIN?

Read Genesis 3:1-5
   a.   Questioning God's word (Verse 1).
   b.   Believing a lie (Verse 4).
   c.   Desiring to be like God (Verse 5).

3. WHAT IS THE RESULT OF SIN?

Read Romans 6:23
   Circle the word that describes the result of ***sin***.

Do you believe people who are guilty of violating the moral law (law of goodness or badness of human action/character) should be punished? So does God! Sin brings God's judgment of death on all who are guilty of breaking God's perfect moral law.

Read Genesis 3:16-24
   Underline every ***result*** of sin you see in these verses.

4. WHO SINS?

Read Romans 3:23
   Circle the word that describes ***who*** God considers a sinner.

Read 1 John 1:8, 10
   Underline the words that describe Christians who ***claim they are without sin*** or have not sinned.

Read Romans 3:10
   Circle the word that indicates ***how many*** people are righteous.

5. HOW DOES SIN HAPPEN?

Read Genesis 3:6
There is a **progression of sin** that we must notice.

SEE ⇨ **TAKE** ⇨ **GIVE**

6. WHAT IS GOD'S SOLUTION FOR SIN?

For thousands of years before Christ, God required that people slay lambs to cover their sins. This was a temporary answer to sin.   Read the Bible passages below that describe God's permanent solution for sin.

Read Colossians 2:13-14.
- *Circle **how many** of our sins God forgave.*
- *Underline what God did with the "**written code**" that contained a list of our sins and the penalty of death.*

The apostle Paul uses an illustration from the legal profession. During his time, convicted criminals were issued a "written code" which listed all the crimes they had committed as well as their penalty sentenced by the court. After fulfilling their sentence, the court took the "written code" and stamped over it the word "***tetelestai***" which in the original language means, "***Paid in Full.***"

Read John 19:30
- *Circle what Jesus said that indicated that **He** had paid our sin debt.*

"**Tetelestai**" was the word Christ used in John 19:30 when He said, *"It is finished,"* just before He died on the cross! Jesus voluntary paid for our sins with His blood by dying on the cross in our place. If Jesus didn't pay for our sins, we would have to.

Read 2 Corinthians 5:21
- *Underline the word that describes what **we become** in Christ.*

❓ Could God have forgiven us without having to sacrifice His Son on the cross? Why or why not?

The death of Jesus Christ satisfies two attributes of God. It satisfies **His Holiness** which required that sin be punished, and it satisfies **His love** which desired man's salvation. Through the sacrifice of Jesus, God is able to demonstrate His love for man while maintaining His Holiness!

7. WHAT SHOULD WE DO WHEN WE SIN?

Read 1 John 1:9

Circle the word that describes **what we must do** when we sin.

The word "**confess**" comes from a word in the original language which means, "to agree with God that we have sinned."

We must understand that confession must be both to **God** and to **any offended person**.

Notice also that 1 John 1:9 is a conditional statement. **If** we confess our sins, God will do two things for us.

Underline those **two** things.

Why does God require us to confess our sins in order to be forgiven?

NOW WHAT?

1. Pray and ask God to reveal any sins which you have not confessed to Him.
2. Confess them to God by agreeing that you have sinned. Don't make excuses for your sins.
3. Turn away from sin and ask God to help you keep from committing them again.
4. Claim the two promises which God makes to those who confess their sins according to 1 John 1:9.
5. Thank God for His forgiveness as an expression of your faith!

Memorize *1 John 1:9*

MORE GOOD NEWS!

The Bible passages below illustrate our forgiveness in 2 different ways.

Read Hebrews 10:17

🖉 Recognizing that God knows all things, what do you think it means when it says "**He will remember our sins no more**"? Write your answer below.

Read Psalms 103:12

❓ How far is the east from the west?

❓ From these verses, how complete is our forgiveness in Christ?

SUGGESTIONS FOR FURTHER EXPLORATION

1. Q: Are all my sins forgiven by God or just the past ones?
   A: Christ died for all our sins: past, present and future.

   Read Hebrews 10:8-18

2. Q: If God has already forgiven all my sins, why then do I have to confess them to Him?
   A: Confession allows you to experience the forgiveness that is already yours in Christ. Sin breaks your fellowship with God, not your relationship with Him. Your relationship with God as His child is based on His unconditional love for you, but your fellowship with Him depends on your keeping an intimate walk with Him. Whereas sin destroys this intimacy, confession restores it!

3. Q: What if I still feel guilty even after confessing?
   A: Any guilt remaining after genuine confession is not from God. Satan, our accuser, delights in keeping us on a guilt trip.

   Read Job 1:1-11
   Read Zechariah 3:1

4. Q: Why should I confess my sins regularly?
   A: Regular confession of our sins keeps our fellowship with God open and fresh. It also keeps our heart sensitive to God's Spirit. Continual sin hardens the heart toward God.

   Read Isaiah 1:15-18

5. Q: What about restitution?
    A: If your sin has hurt others, you should ask their forgiveness, and make restitution if necessary.

    📖 *Read Matthew 5:23-24*

6. Q: How often should I confess my sins?
    A: You should confess as often as necessary. Confess your sins as soon as God convicts you of them. Any delay allows Satan the opportunity to gain a foothold in our lives.

    📖 *Read Ephesians 4:26-27*

7. Q: Will I ever stop sinning?
    A: You will have a constant battle with sin until the day you are with Him.

    📖 *Read Romans 7:15-24*

🙏 PRAYER

Father, I am so sorry for all the many times I have missed the mark. Thank you for paying a debt that I could not pay. I pray that my life would honor you from this day forward. Please help me to take my sin as seriously as you do. Amen.

RECOMMENDED RESOURCES

Book: *Why is there Death & Suffering?* by Ken Ham & Mark Looy

Book: *The Normal Christian Life* by Watchman Nee

FOOTSTEP 3
THE NEW ME

INTRODUCTION

What has changed since I accepted Christ as Savior?

☐ My attitude
☐ My priorities
☐ My bad habits
☐ My spending practices

In this lesson we will discuss what it means to be a new creation in Christ. Thankfully, the story does not stop with Jesus dying on a cross.

Read John 11:25-26
- *Circle **two words** that Jesus claims to be.*
- *Underline what happens if you **believe** in Him.*

   What does it mean to **believe** in Him?

Read Luke 24:1-12

   When the disciples heard the women's story, what did they think about the words of the women?

Read Galatians 2:20
- *Circle **where** Christ lives.*

   How does He accomplish this?

Read John 14:16-17
- *Underline the descriptive word of the **Helper**.*

So, what is Christ doing in me now that I am a follower of Jesus?
Because He is resurrected, I have a *resurrected life.* Let's talk about what a resurrected life looks like.

1. I HAVE A NEW PROMISE

Read Ephesians 1:13-14
- *The Holy Spirit is described as a **seal**. Circle where you see this in the text.*
- *As a seal, underline what He **guarantees**.*

Read 2 Corinthians 5:17

- *Circle* the word that describes you *if* you are *in Christ*.
- *Underline* the *two things* that happen when Christ is in you.

Being a new creation means you...

☐ Grow slowly like an oak tree.
☐ Grow quickly like a weed.
☐ Grow both slowly and quickly.

STOP AND PRAY - Ask the Holy Spirit to conform you to look more like Him in His timing.

2. I AM A NEW PERSON

*"When Jesus comes into our lives, we see **four new things** that a Christian has simply because he is a Christian." Herb Hodges*

A. A Christian Has a New Position

Read John 15: 1-11

- *Underline* every place you see *"in me"* in the first seven verses.

The Christian is "in Christ." When you read the later books of the New Testament, you find the phrase, "in Christ" occurring over and over again. In fact, in Paul's letters alone, the phrase "in Christ" is used **164 times** to define the Christian's new position.

In order to understand our new position "in Christ," we must understand our old position before we trusted Christ.

An adopted child in a new family has a new position.

Read 1 Corinthians 15:22

- *Circle* the *two positions* that represent all mankind.

B. A Christian Has a New Possession

Read John 15:4-5

- *Circle where* Christ dwells.

Read Colossians 1:27

❓ What is the answer to the age-old mystery of, "How can we really know God?" *Circle this answer in the text.*

Since He lives in me, I will only find true personal fulfillment as I live in union **with** Him. He came into me for a reason. **With** Him, I am able to do what I simply cannot do without Him.

C. A Christian Has a New Product

Read John 15:1-8

✎ Place a *rectangle* around every time you see "***fruit***" in verses 1-8.

The new product of a Christian's life is to ***produce fruit.***

❓ What is fruit?

Fruit is a natural product of a healthy vine. You do not have to command a grape vine to bear grapes, or an apple tree to bear apples. If these plants are healthy, they naturally bear fruit after their own kind. Fruit-bearing is an effortless thing. When the branch abides in the vine, the natural product is fruit.

Fruit has the **flavor** of the vine that bears it, and the Christian is to have the **flavor** of Jesus Christ in his life. Jesus does not want you to work for Him; He wants you to let Him do His best through you. This is fruit – Jesus Christ "producing" His life and character and works in and through you.

Types of fruit:
1. Character fruit

Read Galatians 5:22-23

God's character is revealed in a believer's life.

2. Convert fruit

Read John 15:16

God using you to produce other Christians.

3. Conduct fruit

Read Colossians 1:10

Read Philippians 1:9-11

Christ's conduct is produced in your life – both *negatively* and *positively*.

4. **Contribution fruit**

Read Philippians 4:13-19

Read Romans 15:25-28

Eternally investing your money and resources.

5. **Confessional fruit**

Read Hebrews 13:15

Using your daily speech to praise Jesus and bear testimony to Him.

By the fruit which Christians bear, the world judges both the Vine and the branches. The Christian is to bear fruit; this is the new product of the Christian life!

D. **A Christian Has a New Purpose**

Read John 15:1-11

> Place a *bracket* around "**abide**" or "**remain**" in these verses.

In this entire text, there is exactly one command: To **abide** or **remain** in Him.

I am to keep the point of contact between me and Jesus Christ intact at all times. The most vital part of the branch is the small area where the vine and the branch connect. The only real concern of the Christian is to be sure that he "abides" in Christ. To abide in Christ is to deliberately set aside my own merit, my own wisdom, my own strength, my own resources, in order to draw all from Him.

Read 1 John 2:28

> *Circle* the phase that ***prevents*** us from being ashamed before Christ.

3. **I HAVE A NEW POWER**

How do these changes happen? How do you get a new promise? How do you become a new person? How do you produce fruit?

Read Acts 1:8

> *Circle* **what** the Spirit brings when He comes into you.

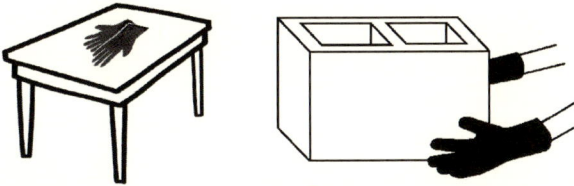

The gloves on the table are *useless* to do work on their own. It is only when someone puts his or her fingers in them that they becomes animated and are able to accomplish a task. In the same way, we are *useless* in our flesh for His kingdom. It is only when we allow the Holy Spirit to **fill us** and to utilize **His power** that work will be accomplished.

I have a *new power* available to me, but will I *allow Him* to completely fill me and display His power through me?

NOW WHAT?
1. Knowing the importance of **abiding** in Christ, would you say that you are currently abiding in Him?
    ☐ **Yes** ☐ **No**
2. Identify any distractions in your life that are separating you from truly **abiding** completely in Him.
3. Pray for the Holy Spirit to fill you completely so that He will be able to display His power through you.

 Memorize Acts 1:8

PRAYER
Father, I thank You for the new me! Thank you for depositing the Holy Spirit within me. Help me to grow into maturity so that I will look like Jesus. I pray that I would understand the responsibilities of being in Your family. Please mold me in a way that You will bear much fruit from my life. Amen.

RECOMMENDED RESOURCES

Book: *The Complete Green Letters* by Miles Stanford

Video: Road to Emmaus
www.roadtoemmausmovie.com

"The Word of God is the fulcrum upon which the lever of prayer is placed, and by which things are mightily moved."

-E. M. Bounds

FOOTSTEP 4
COMMUNICATION WITH GOD:
PRAYER AND STUDYING MY BIBLE

INTRODUCTION

How long do you think you can survive without eating?

- ☐ 1 day
- ☐ 10 days
- ☐ 20 days
- ☐ 40 days
- ☐ 60 days
- ☐ 100 days

If you marked 1 day, you have never missed a meal in your life! No, it's not even 10 or 20 days. We can survive 40 days without food, but after that, our bodies begin to starve and death is not far off. Just as our physical bodies need food to grow and survive, even so, our spirit needs to be fed as well. Notice how the metaphor (image) of milk and solid food is used in Scripture.

Why should you crave pure spiritual milk?

Read 1 Peter 2:2
Circle what happens when you ***crave pure spiritual milk***.

Read Colossians 2:6-7
We are to walk in Christ in the ***very same manner*** that we received Him. *Circle "**as**" or "**just as**"* in verse 6.
As we are being built up in Christ, what should be overflowing from our lives? *Underline* the ***answer*** in the text.

Read 1 Thessalonians 5:18
Underline the ***command*** in this verse.
We must spend time thanking Him for spiritual blessings, people, and material blessings.

In order to spiritually survive, we must learn to communicate with God. There are two ways in which this happens: Prayer and studying our Bible.

WE COMMUNICATE WITH HIM THROUGH PRAYER

1. **Jesus set the example of prayer for His disciples.**

   Read Mark 1:35
   Circle what Jesus was ***doing*** in a secluded place.

? Why would Jesus need to pray? Isn't He God?

2. **Jesus taught them that prayer was a necessity.**

    Read Luke 18:1
    - *Underline* the **purpose** of the parable found in Luke 18:1-8.

3. **Jesus' disciples asked Him how to pray.**

    Read Luke 11:1
    - *Underline* what Jesus was **doing** in this verse.
    - *Circle* what His disciples **asked** Jesus to do.

    ? Growing up, what was your experience with prayer? Did someone teach you how to pray?

4. **Jesus wants constant communication with His disciples.**

    Read 1 Thessalonians 5:17
    - *Circle* how **often** we should pray.

    ? What does this look like?

LEARNING HOW TO PRAY

In Matthew 6:9-13, Jesus gave us a model for our prayers. In this lesson, we have put these verses from the Holman translation and we will look at each phrase individually.

1. **"Our Father who is in heaven"**
   We have a personal relationship with the greatest authority in the Universe.

    Read Romans 8:15-17
    - *Underline* the type of **spirit** we receive from God.
    - *Circle* what we may **cry out** to Him.

2. **"Your name be honored as holy"**
   When you recognize His character, it is only natural to give Him adoration.

    Read Revelation 4:8, 11

📖 *Read Psalm 145:3*
  ✎ *Underline* the words that describe God's **character**.

3. **"Your kingdom come. Your will be done on earth as it is in heaven."**
God has a preferred will. This is your agreement to do His will rather than your own.

📖 *Read Luke 22:42*
  ✎ *Circle* whose **will** Jesus was submitting to in this verse.

4. **"Give us today our daily bread"**
This portion of the prayer is asking Him for your physical provisions.

📖 *Read Matthew 6:24-34*
  ✎ *Circle* each place you see "**worry**" or "**anxious**" in these verses.
  ✎ Place a *rectangle* around the word "**but**" in verse 33.
  ✎ *Underline* God's **solution for worry** found in verse 33.

5. **"And forgive us our debts, as we also have forgiven our debtors"**
You must confess that you miss the mark.

📖 *Read Psalm 66:18*
  ✎ *Underline* why we must **confess** to Him.
📖 *Read Luke 5:8*
  ✎ *Circle* the reason Simon Peter wanted Jesus to get **away** from Him.
📖 *Read 1 John 1:9*

6. **"And do not bring us into temptation, but deliver us from the evil one"**
You must trust Him for power over temptation.

📖 *Read 1 Corinthians 10:13*
  ✎ *Circle* what God provides during **temptation**.

7. **"For Yours is the kingdom and the power and the glory forever. Amen"**
In Jesus' model prayer, He finishes with adoration, just like He began. Acknowledging His character is obviously important in our prayers!

🛑 **STOP AND PRAY USING JESUS' MODEL PRAYER AS YOUR GUIDE.**

WE COMMUNICATE WITH HIM THROUGH STUDYING OUR BIBLE

Currently, do you have a time that you sit down and read your Bible? If so, when and where do you have your time with the Lord?

Read 2 Peter 3:14-18

Underline the description of some parts of **Scripture** found in verse 16.

Circle the **two adjectives** of those who distort Scripture.

Read Colossians 2:6-7

We must understand the basics or we will have a faulty foundation!

Read 2 Timothy 2:15

Circle the word that describes **how** we are to read Scripture.

Once we understand the basics of studying God's word, we must do our best to learn how to handle His word.

LEARNING HOW TO STUDY – THE INTERPRETIVE JOURNEY

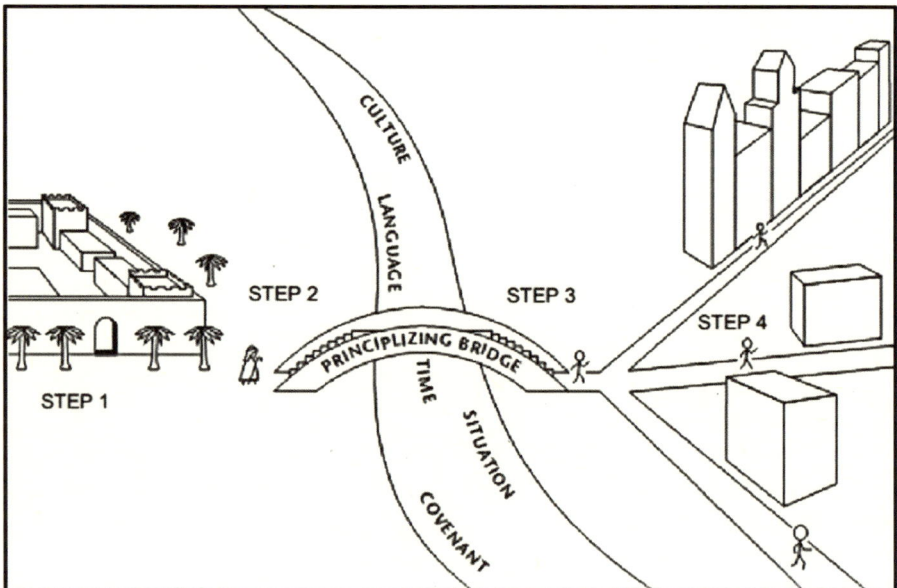

Step 1: Grasp the text in their town.

What did the text mean to the original audience?

Read the text carefully and try to see as much as possible in the text.

The Bible was not written <u>to</u> us, but was written <u>for</u> us.

a. Identify to whom the text was written.

b. Look for repeated words.

c. Look for significant words.

d. Determine the historical context (What was going on?).

e. Find the relation to surrounding text.

Step 2: Measure the width of the river to cross.

What are the differences between the biblical audience and us?

We are separated from the biblical audience by:

a. Culture

b. Language

c. Situation

d. Time

e. Covenant

Picture these differences as a river that hinders us from moving straight from the meaning in their context to the meaning in ours.

It is important to know just how wide the river is before we try to build a principlizing bridge across it.

Step 3: Cross the Principlizing Bridge.

What are the theological principle(s) in this text?

Look for the theological principle or principles that are reflected in the meaning of the text you identified in Step 1. This theological principle is part of the meaning. Your task is not to create the meaning but to **discover** the meaning intended by the author. Remember, it was not written to us, it was written to them, but God **preserved** it for us.

a. The principle should be reflected in the text.

b. The principle should be timeless and not tied to a specific situation.

c. The principle should not be culturally bound.

d. The principle should agree with the teaching of the rest of Scripture.

e. The principle should be relevant to both the biblical audience and us.

Step 4: Grasp the text in our town.

How should I live out the theological principles?

For each passage, there will usually be only a few (and often only one) theological principles relevant for Christians today, but there will be numerous application possibilities. This is because we find ourselves in many different specific situations.

Each of us will grasp and apply the same theological principle in slightly different ways, depending on our current life situation and where we are in our relationship with God. Trust the Holy Spirit and allow Him to reveal areas in your life that need to be corrected so that you will look more like Jesus.

NOW WHAT?

Using your notes from each step of the Interpretive Journey, what are the key elements found in the following passage?

Read Acts 8:25-40

Step 1: Grasp the text in their town.

What did the text mean to the original audience?
a. Identify to whom the text was written:

b. Look for repeated words:

c. Look for significant words:

d. Determine the historical context (What was going on?):

e. Find the relation to surrounding text:

Step 2: Measure the width of the river to cross.

What are the differences between the biblical audience and us?
a. Culture:

b. Language:

    c.   Situation:

    d.   Time:

    e.   Covenant:

Step 3: Cross the Principlizing Bridge.

What are the theological principle(s) in this text?
    a.   What principles are reflected in this text?

    b.   Are these principles timeless?

    c.   Are these principles tied to culture?

    d.   Are these principles consistent with the rest of Scripture?

    e.   Are these principles relevant to both the biblical audience and us?

Step 4: Grasp the text in our town.

How should I live out the theological principles?

Memorize *Matthew 6:9-13*

Memorize *2 Timothy 2:15*

SUGGESTIONS FOR FURTHER EXPLORATION

There is another method that can help when studying specific passages in Scripture. As you read a passage, look for the following:

1. **Promises to claim**
2. **Commands to obey**
3. **Sins to forsake**
4. **Blessings to enjoy**
5. **Prayers to echo**
6. **Examples to follow**
7. **Teachings to learn**

PRAYER

Father, thank You for Your word. I pray for an intense hunger for Your word. Please teach me what it means to study diligently. I pray for the Holy Spirit to bring clarity as I study and that I would apply the principles accurately in my life. Amen.

RECOMMENDED RESOURCES

Book: *The Attributes of God* by Arthur W. Pink

Book: *The Prayer-Shaped Disciple* by Dan Crawford

Book: *Holman Illustrated Bible Handbook* by B & H Editorial

Book: *Grasping God's Word* by J. Scott Duvall & J. Daniel Hayes

Software: *The Discovery Bible*
www.thediscoverybible.com

FOOTSTEP 5
PUBLICLY DECLARING MY FAITH:
BAPTISM AND TESTIMONY

INTRODUCTION

? **What do you think is the greatest threat to Christianity?**

☐ Ungodly people
☐ Our culture
☐ Antagonistic government

Someone once said...

> *"The greatest threat to Christianity is Christians trying to sneak into heaven without ever sharing their faith."*

We have the *privilege* as God's children to invite others to be reconciled with God! *There is no greater decision people can make than trusting Jesus Christ as their personal Savior and Lord.*

? How could Christians not sharing their faith be the *greatest* threat to Christianity?

? Why do you think many Christians do not share their faith?

WE CAN SHARE OUR FAITH THROUGH BAPTISM

1. **Baptism is a public declaration of our faith in Jesus.**

   Read Matthew 10:32-33
   - *Circle* what Jesus commands us to do **before men**.
   - *Underline* what we must **not** do before men.

2. **Baptism doesn't make us clean. It shows that we are clean.**

   Read Matthew 3:13-17
   - *Underline* the **reason** Jesus was baptized according to verse 15.

3. **Baptism is a standard practice for new believers.**

   Read Acts 2:37-38
   - *Circle* the **two actions** Peter instructs those who believe in Jesus to do.

31

4. **Baptism pictures six things.**

📖 *Read Romans 6:1-4*

    a. Baptism shows our **position**.
       ✏ *Circle* "***baptized into Christ Jesus***" in verse 3.

    b. Baptism shows our **funeral**.
       ✏ *Underline* what else we were ***baptized into*** according to verse 3.

    c. Baptism shows our **new purpose**.
       ✏ Place a *rectangle* around "***in order that***" or "***so that***" in verse 4.

    d. Baptism shows our **new example**.
       ✏ *Circle* the **phrase** that indicates your new example according to verse 4.

    e. Baptism shows our **new available strength**.
       ✏ *Underline* how Jesus was ***raised from the dead***.

    f. Baptism shows our **new journey**.
       ✏ Place a *rectangle* around how we are to ***conduct our lives*** after we are baptized.

WE CAN SHARE OUR FAITH THROUGH OUR TESTIMONY

📖 *Read Matthew 4:18-22*
    ✏ *Underline* Jesus' **invitation** to the fishermen.
    ✏ *Circle* their **action** as they followed Jesus (Verse 20).

These guys had a choice to make. Were they going to hold on to their old life or were they going to follow Him? If they followed Him, they would spend the rest of their lives **fishing for men**.

Your **testimony** is the tool you use to **fish for men**.

📖 *Read Matthew 5:14-16*
    ✏ *Underline* Jesus' **description** of you in verse 14.
    ✏ *Circle* who is **glorified** when we let our light shine.

1. **In order to share our testimony, we must be available.**

📖 *Read Matthew 9:37*
    ✏ *Underline* the word that described the ***amount of workers*** available for the harvest.

2. **In order to share our testimony, we must be prayerful.**

   Read Matthew 9:38
   Circle what Jesus's disciples were to ***pray for*** in this verse.

3. **In order to share our testimony, we must be filled with the Spirit.**

   Read Matthew 10:20
   Circle **who** speaks in us.

4. **In order to share our testimony, we must be mindful of our responsibility and His responsibility.**

   Read John 6:44
   Underline the ***only way*** a person is able to come to Jesus.

HOW TO SHARE YOUR TESTIMONY

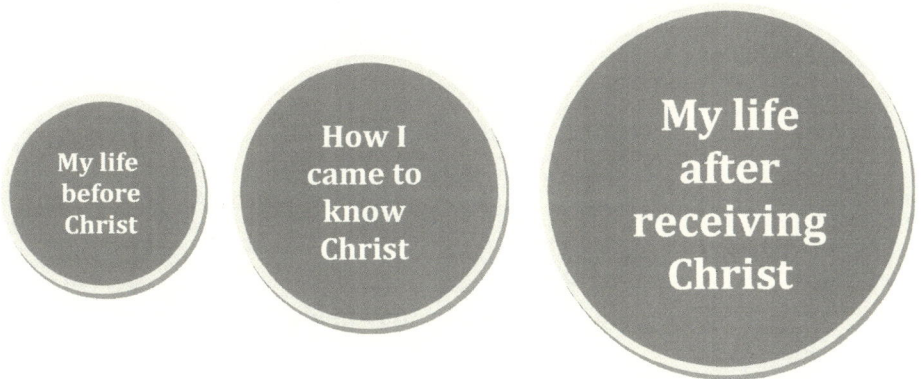

My life before Christ

How I came to know Christ

My life after receiving Christ

When you share your testimony, your life before Christ is a very small portion. This is where you begin, but do not dwell there.

A larger portion of your testimony should consist of how you came to know Christ. Be as specific as possible in this portion of your testimony.

By far, the largest portion of your testimony should focus on how He has changed you. This portion should *always* be changing because God is always *active*.

NOW WHAT?

❓ What do we need to do to prepare for your baptism?

Write your testimony on a separate sheet of paper. Make sure to include all three elements we discussed in this lesson.

Pick 5 people who don't have a relationship with Jesus to tell your story to.

1. _____

? _____

3. _____

4. _____

5. _____

Memorize *Matthew 9:37-38*

PRAYER

Father, guard my heart that I do not become indifferent about those people around me who are lost and without hope. Prompt me to take advantage of every opportunity that You give me and be Your witness by telling others my story and what You rescued me and how You can do the same thing for them. Amen.

RECOMMENDED RESOURCES

Book: *Baptism: What Can We Agree On?* by RBC Ministries

Book: *Share Jesus Without Fear* by William Fay

FOOTSTEP 6
OUR JOURNEY TOGETHER:
FELLOWSHIP AND WORSHIP

INTRODUCTION
A baby is born. Ten years later, it is still the *same size* and *maturity* as when it was born. Your immediate reaction is:

- ☐ *"Wow, He's still so cute!"*
- ☐ *"Well...I guess some babies grow slower than others."*
- ☐ *"Get this kid to a doctor...NOW!"*

It doesn't take a *doctor* to figure out that the baby in our story is not normal. Normal babies **grow** and **mature.** It is *abnormal* not to!

When God placed His *Holy Spirit* in you at the moment you trusted Christ for forgiveness, you were spiritually *"born again"*. *Instantly*, you became a **member of God's eternal family**, a *new creation* in Christ, created to *grow* to maturity and *destined to glorify Christ* through your life.

📖 *Read 2 Peter 3:18*
    ✎ *Underline* what a believer must **grow in** as stated in this verse.

OUR JOURNEY TOGETHER INVOLVES FELLOWSHIP
❓ **Why do I need a church?**

🚶 1. **In the local church, we receive instruction.**

    📖 *Read Ephesians 4:11-14*
    ✎ *Underline* the **reason** God gave leaders to the church.

    My job is to be **willing** to learn everything my pastor and teacher pours into me so that I will be able to handle God's Word accurately and so that I will be ready for my God-given assignments.

2. **In the local church, we have the privilege of fellowship.**

    📖 *Read Hebrews 10:24-25*
    ✎ *Circle* the word that describes what we are to do to **one another** found in verse 24.

In the original language, this word is *paroksysmós* which literally means to jab someone so that they **must respond.**

> *"Father, make of me a crisis man. Bring those I contact to decision. Let me not be a milepost on a single road; make me a fork, that men must turn one way or another on facing Christ in me." Jim Elliott*

✐ *Underline* what we are **not** to do according to verse 25.

❓ What does the word **fellowship**◪ mean?

❓ Why do we need this fellowship?

3. In the local church, we have opportunities for service.

📖 *Read Romans 12:6-8*
   ✐ *Underline* the reason we each have **different gifts**.

You have special gifts and abilities that God expects you to use! God has given **all believers** spiritual gifts. They are NOT talents. They are NOT skills. They are *gifts*.

❓ What are my spiritual gifts?

📖 *Read 1 Corinthians 12:18-20*
   ✐ *Circle* the **repeated words** in these verses.

📖 *Read Ephesians 2:10*
   ✐ *Circle* the **descriptive word** of us found in this verse.

4. In the local church, we engage in corporate worship.

📖 *Read Colossians 3:16*
   ✐ *Underline* the **two actions** we are to do to one another as we meet together.
   ✐ *Circle* what the **word of Christ** is to do within us.

Read 1 Corinthians 14:26

Circle who is to **participate** in worship as the church gathers together.

OUR JOURNEY TOGETHER INVOLVES WORSHIP

What is worship?

Worship is God revealing Himself or His ways and our responding appropriately to Him.

> *"Your view of God is the most important view you have and to the degree it is distorted, to that degree your life is out of focus." Gordon Borror*

1. Worship is both private and corporate.

Read Romans 1:28

Circle the word God uses to describe the **type of mind** He will turn them over to if they do not acknowledge Him.

This word means someone who does **not** act on truth. We must become soft in heart so, when God speaks, we are ready to respond.

2. Worship is expressive.

Read Psalms 47:1

Underline the **emotional** words in this verse.

Read Matthew 26:6-13

Underline **verse 13**.

3. Worship is costly.

Read 2 Samuel 24:18-25

Underline **verse 24**.

Read Matthew 27:57-60

Circle the words that describe **Jesus' tomb** in verse 60.

4. **Worship is authentic.**

Read Acts 5:1-6

Circle who Ananias **lied to** in verse 3.

NOW WHAT?

Identify your spiritual gifts. List these gifts below:

What should I look for in a local church?
- A pastor that is *available*.
- A pastor that *equips* you.
- A church with a *correct doctrine*.
- A church that is actively looking to *reach the world* for Christ.

Memorize *Ephesians 2:10*

PRAYER

Father, thank You for the gifts You have blessed me with. I pray that I will use them as the tools You designed them to be. I also pray for a sensitive heart that is ready to worship You. Amen.

RECOMMENDED RESOURCES

Book: *I Am a Church Member* by Thom Rainer

Book: *Explaining Worship* by Jack Hayford

FOOTSTEP 7
UNDERSTANDING MY PRIZE:
MY CURRENT GIFT AND MY FUTURE REWARDS

INTRODUCTION

Which of these is a gift?

- [ ] A bonus at work
- [ ] A birthday present
- [ ] An Olympic gold medal
- [ ] Speeding ticket

There is a huge difference between a **gift** and a **reward**. Salvation is a gift. It is guaranteed by the grace of God to those who receive Christ by faith. Rewards, on the other hand, are given for obedience to the Lord's instructions. They are not guaranteed, but only obtained by true submission to Jesus Christ.

THE GIFT	REWARDS

1) **Salvation is the free gift and cannot be earned.**
 	
Read Romans 5:15-16
   Circle the **repeated** word.
 	
If someone offers you a free gift, do you have to pay for it?
   [ ] YES [ ] NO
 	
Read Ephesians 2:8-9
   Circle what **saved** you.
   Underline what did **not** save you.
 	
Read Romans 6:23
What is the free gift of God?
	1) **Rewards can be earned by faithful service.**
	
	Read Colossians 3:22-24
	   Underline what you will receive **if** you serve the Lord heartily.
	
	Note that the emphasis of this passage is upon **service**.
	
	Read Revelation 22:12
	   Underline the **basis** of our rewards.

🎁 THE GIFT	🏆 REWARDS

2) Salvation is not something we deserve.
 	
❓ If God were to give us exactly what we deserve for the way we have lived and for the sins which we have committed, what would He give us?
 	
📖 *Read Titus 3:4-7*
  ✏️ *Circle* the words that describe God's **character**.
  ✏️ *Underline* what stands in **contrast** to His mercy and does **not** save.
📖 *Read Psalm 103:10*
  ✏️ *Underline* this verse.
	2) Rewards are something a believer deserves.
	
	There are two words used in the original language for "rewards."
	
	a. ***Misthos*: A wage** that appropriately compensates a particular decision or action.
	  📖 *Read Luke 6:23*
	  ✏️ *Circle* the word **"reward."**
	  📖 *Read Romans 4:4*
	  ✏️ *Underline* how a wage is **credited**.
	
	b. ***Apodidomai* – A repayment** for expenses incurred as a result of following Jesus.
	  📖 *Read Luke 14:13-14*
	  ✏️ *Circle* what **will happen** at the resurrection of the righteous.
	  📖 *Read Mark 9:41*

3) Salvation is a present possession (as a believer, we have it now).
 	
📖 *Read John 5:24*
❓ Does a believer have eternal life now?
  ☐ YES ☐ NO
📖 *Read 1 John 5:12*
  ✏️ *Circle* what a person **has** if they have the Son.
	3) Rewards are a future attainment (as a believer, we will receive these later).
	
	📖 *Read Luke 14:13-14*
	  ✏️ *Underline* **when** you will be repaid.

🎁 **THE GIFT**	🏆 **REWARDS**
4) Salvation is something that we can never lose. 📖 *Read John 10:27-28* ✎ *Underline* the **two things** that will NOT happen to a believer.	**4) Rewards can be lost.** 📖 *Read 2 John 8* ❓ Why do you need to watch yourself?

📖 *Read 1 Corinthians 3:14-15*
  ✎ *Circle* where there will be **loss of reward**.
  ✎ *Underline* where there is **not** a **loss of salvation**.

| **5) Salvation is based upon what Christ has done.**

📖 *Read Romans 3:24*
✎ *Circle* **where** your redemption is found. | **5) Rewards are based upon what we have done (as a believer).**

📖 *Read 2 Corinthians 5:10*
✎ *Underline* what our judgment will be **based upon** when we appear before Christ. |
| **6) The question of salvation: DID WE *BELIEVE* ON CHRIST?**
📖 *Read Acts 16:31*
✎ *Underline* how you are **saved**. | **6) The question of rewards: DID WE *BUILD* ON CHRIST?**
📖 *Read 1 Corinthians 3:11-14*
✎ *Circle* our **foundation**.
✎ *Underline* what the **fire** will test.
❓ It is easy to be busy **for** Him; but are the things I am doing **from** Him? |

THE GIFT	REWARDS
7) When it comes to salvation there are certain things that God does not remember. 📖 *Read Hebrews 10:17.* ✎ *Circle* the things that God does ***not remember***.	7) When it comes to rewards, there are certain things that God does remember. 📖 *Read Hebrews 6:10.* ✎ *Underline* the ***two things*** that God does not forget.
8) All believers share the same salvation. 📖 *Read Ephesians 1:3* ✎ *Underline* what we ***possess***.	8) All believers do not share the same rewards. 📖 *Read Matthew 16:27* Here Jesus quotes Psalm 62:12. 📖 *Read Psalm 62:12* ✎ *Circle* what determines the ***degree*** of our rewards found in each verse.

NOW WHAT?
1. It is easy to be busy **for** Him, but are the things you are doing **from** Him? Identify what things you are currently doing that are **not** from Him and recognize that these things have no eternal value.
2. Pray for sensitivity to His voice and a heart ready to obey.
3. Thank Him for His amazing gift of salvation.

🌳 ***Memorize** Psalm 103:10*

SUGGESTIONS FOR FURTHER EXPLORATION

1. **Will I not be satisfied with simply being in Heaven?**

   📖 *Read 1 Corinthians 13:12*

   There is a reason that He offers rewards. One day, you will know Him to the extent that you have been known.

📖 *Read 1 Corinthians 15:41-42*

> Just as stars differ from one another in glory, **believers** will differ from one another in Heaven.

2. **What are the things for which God will reward me?**
   (from *A Life God Rewards* by Bruce Wilkinson with David Kopp)
   a. God will reward you for **seeking Him** through spiritual acts such as fasting and praying (Matthew 6:6; Hebrews 11:6).
   b. God will reward you for **submitting** to your employer as a faithful steward (Matthew 24:45-47; Ephesians 6:8; Colossians 3:22-24).
   c. God will reward you for **self-denial** in His service (Matthew 16:24-27).
   d. God will reward you for **serving** those in need in His name (Mark 9:41).
   e. God will reward you for **suffering** for His name and reputation (Luke 6:22-23).
   f. God will reward you for **sacrifices** you make for Him (Luke 6:35). In fact, Jesus said that every person who sacrifices to follow Him will be rewarded a hundredfold (Matthew 19:29)!
   g. God will reward you for **sharing** of your time, talent, and treasure to further His kingdom (Matthew 6:3-4; 1 Timothy 6:18-19).

3. **What is the key to living a life worthy of rewards?**

   📖 *Read Philippians 3:12-14*

   📖 *Read 1 Corinthians 9:24*

🙏 **PRAYER**

Father, thank You so much for the free gift of salvation. I am amazed at Your intense love for me. Please teach me what it means to follow You fully. While I know my eternal destiny will be with You, my prayer is that I will be mature on that day. Keep me sensitive to Your voice and ready to act on Your instructions. Amen.

RECOMMENDED RESOURCES

Book: *Heaven* by Randy Alcorn

Book: *A Life God Rewards* by Bruce Wilkinson with David Kopp

Audio CD: *Affabel: Window of Eternity* by John Bevere

DVD: "Run! The Passion of Elijah" in *Faith Lessons, Volume 7: Walk as Jesus Walked* by Ray Vander Laan

"There is nothing wrong with men possessing riches. The wrong comes when riches possess men."

-Billy Graham

FOOTSTEP 8
TAKING CARE OF BUSINESS

INTRODUCTION

Which of the following describes stewardship?

- [ ] Using our money wisely.
- [ ] Using our time wisely.
- [ ] Using our spiritual gifts wisely.
- [ ] All the above.

Stewardship is utilizing and managing all resources God provides for the glory of God and the betterment of His creation. It involves much more than just **money**. In this lesson, we will look at what it means to be a good steward for Jesus.

1. **Everything belongs to God to begin with!**

   Read Psalm 24:1-2
   Circle who owns the earth and **everything** in it.

   Read Ecclesiastes 2:17-22
   Underline who gets the **fruit** of our earthly labor in verse 18.

2. **Everything we have in our possession, He has entrusted to us.**

   Read Matthew 25:14-18
   Circle the number of **talents** each slave received.

   a. Our **time** has been entrusted to us.

      Read Ephesians 5:15-16
      Underline what we are to do with our **time**.

      Read Psalm 90:12
      Circle what the Psalmist asks God to **teach**.

   b. Our **money** has been entrusted to us.

      Read Deuteronomy 8:17-18
      Circle where our **wealth** comes from.
      Underline how He **gives you** wealth.
      Read Malachi 3:8
      Circle two ways we can **rob** God.

45

Read Malachi 1:6-11

- *Circle* how God views ***substandard offerings*** in verse 8.
- *Underline* why God demands a ***pure offering*** in verse 11.

c. Our **spiritual gifts** have been entrusted to us.

Read Romans 12:6-8

Read 1 Corinthians 7:7

- *Underline* how each of us ***differ***.

Read 1 Peter 4:10

- *Circle* what each of us ***receive***.
- *Underline* what we are to ***do*** with it.

d. Our **relationships** have been entrusted to us.

Read 2 Corinthians 5:18-21

- *Circle* the ***type of ministry*** God gave each of us when He saved us.
- *Circle* our ***job description*** found in verse 20.

e. Our **body** has been entrusted to us.

Read 1 Corinthians 3:16-17

- *Circle* the word that ***describes*** our body in verse 16.
- *Underline* who ***dwells*** in us.

Read 1 Corinthians 6:19-20

- *Underline* the ***description*** of your body.
- *Circle* what you are to ***do*** with your body.

f. Our **possessions** have been entrusted to us.

Read James 1:16-17

- *Circle* where ***every*** good thing comes from.

g.   Our **words** have been entrusted to us.

Read 1 Timothy 6:20-21
Underline what Timothy was to **avoid**.

Read Ephesians 4:29
Circle what should **not** come out of our mouth.
Underline what **should** come out of our mouth.

Read 1 Peter 4:11
Circle the phrase that should describe the **origin** of our speech.

3. **He expects a return on what He has entrusted to us.**

Read Matthew 25:19-30
Circle the action of the master when he **returned** to the slaves in verse 19.
Underline how the master describes the slave that **does not** invest in verse 30.

Read 2 Thessalonians 3:10
The return on His investment necessitates you *working*.

Read Ephesians 4:28
Underline the **reason** we are to work.

4. **There will be a day when we must give an account for His investments.**

Read 1 Corinthians 3:1-15
Underline the **repeated phrase** in verses 6 and 7.
Circle what we **receive** according to our labor in verse 8.

Read Matthew 12:36-37
Circle the **two options** for our words.

Read 1 Timothy 6:17-19
Circle where we are to **fix our hope**.
Underline what we **store for ourselves** in Heaven if we invest wisely.

NOW WHAT?

? Look at your time, money, spiritual gifts, relationships, body, possessions, and words. Right now, would you say that they are expenditure or an *investment*?

	Expenditure	Investment
Time		
Money		
Spiritual Gifts		
Relationships		
Body		
Possessions		
Words		

? In what specific ways can you begin to *invest* each of these things?

a. **Time:**

b. **Money:**

c. **Spiritual Gifts:**

d. **Relationships:**

e. **Body:**

f. **Possessions:**

g. **Words:**

Memorize James 1:16-17

Prayer

Father, I know that everything belongs to You. Thank you so much for entrusting me with Your possessions. Please help me to understand the importance of investing everything you have blessed me with for Your kingdom. May I be found faithful to invest my time, money, spiritual gifts, relationships, body, possessions, and words wisely. Amen.

RECOMMENDED RESOURCES

Book: *Raising a Modern-Day Knight* by Robert Lewis

Book: *Raising a Modern-Day Princess* by Doreen Hanna & Pam Farrel

Book: *This Momentary Marriage* by John Piper

"God has not promised to bless our good motives, dreams and innovations. He has promised to bless His plan, that plan is that disciples make other disciples – everything else is a side show."

-Bill Hull

FOOTSTEP 9
MY MARCHING ORDERS

INTRODUCTION
HOW WOULD YOU ANSWER THE FOLLOWING?

Why am I here instead of in heaven?

- ☐ Because my home in heaven is not finished yet.
- ☐ Because I must not be good enough yet.
- ☐ Because God is having second thoughts about me.
- ☐ None of the above.

Read Philippians 1:21-24
- *Circle what would be **produced** if Paul continued to live.*
- *Underline who would **benefit** if Paul continued to live.*

1. I HAVE A COMMAND TO HEAR

Read Matthew 28:18-20

There is only **one** imperative command in the commission.

Which word is the command?
- *Circle the **command**.*
- *Underline the other verb forms that tell you **how** to accomplish your command to make disciples.*

2. I HAVE DEFINITIONS TO UNDERSTAND

a. Disciple

Disciples are both the people who please the Lord and the people who will reach the world.

A disciple is a committed, lifelong learner and follower of Jesus Christ.

b. Discipler

A discipler, or disciple-maker, is a person who "turns men into disciples."

By definition, a discipler must have a disciple.

c. Disciple-Making

Disciple-making, or discipling, is the process of building men and women into disciples.

Disciple-making is done by *someone, not by something*. It is done by *persons, not by programs*. It is accomplished by *individuals, not by institutions.*

Technically, discipling is one Christian person imparting his whole life to another, by example, leadership, and relationship.

Disciple-making is more than a class. It is life transference.

d. **Disciplines** ▦

Disciplines are the areas of life that reveal the cost of discipleship. Among others, disciplines include studying your Bible, praying, memorizing Scripture, fellowshipping with other believers, fasting, and being a good steward of His resources.

Disciplines are a necessary part of being a disciple of Jesus.

3. I HAVE A STRATEGY TO USE

What is the difference between spiritual addition and spiritual multiplication? Let's say a person preached to large crowds and 100 people accepted Christ each day. In contrast, let's say a person won one person to Christ and discipled him or her for 6 months. At the end of that 6 months, each person won one more to Christ and discipled that person for 6 months. The process continued with a new disciple every 6 months. Which method would make the greatest impact?

Spiritual Addition	Year	Spiritual Multiplication
(Reach 100 people for Christ each day)		(Win, build & send one person every 6 months)
36,000	1	4
72,000	2	16
108,000	3	64
144,000	4	256
180,000	5	1,024
216,000	6	4,069
252,000	7	16,384
288,000	8	65,536
324,000	9	262,144
360,000	10	1,048,576
396,000	11	16,777,216
432,000	12	67,108,864
468,000	13	268,435,456
504,000	14	1,073,741,824
540,000	15	4,294,967,296
576,000	16	17,179,867,184

Read 2 Timothy 2:2

How many generations are represented in this verse?

Spiritual Multiplication is diagramed at right. Notice that each succeeding generation grows as those who have learned now teach others. This is the magic of Spiritual Multiplication.

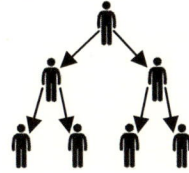

---

4. I HAVE A CURRICULUM TO FOLLOW

Read 2 Timothy 1:13
   Circle what Paul instructs Timothy to **keep**.

While we must *teach* our disciples, it must **not** be limited to a classroom.

Read Mark 3:14
   Circle the **first reason** Jesus appointed His disciples.

Read John 3:22
   Underline what Jesus was **doing** with His disciples.

"Spending time" literally means *to rub your character into another*.

Read 2 Timothy 3:10-11

Paul tells Timothy that he had taught him **nine** things. What are these nine things?

1. _____

2. _____

   Read Philippians 3:17
      Circle what Paul tells the Philippians to **follow**.

   Read 1 Corinthians 11:1
      Underline who Paul tells the Corinthians to **imitate**.
      Circle who Paul **imitates**.

❓ Right now, are you able to pull someone close to you and tell them to ***follow your example*** so that they will ***look like Christ***?

☐ **Yes** ☐ **No**

3. _____

📖 *Read Romans 15:20*

🖊 *Underline* where Paul did ***not*** aspire to preach the gospel.

📖 *Read 1 Corinthians 3:10*

🖊 *Circle* Paul's role in ***building*** the Corinthians.

❓ What is your life's purpose? What has God made you passionate about?

4. _____

📖 *Read Acts 9:5-6*

🖊 *Underline* the ***faith statement***.

📖 *Read Acts 16:6*

🖊 *Circle* what the Holy Spirit ***forbid*** Paul to do in Asia.

📖 *Read Acts 18:9*

🖊 *Underline* the ***faith statement***.

5. _____

📖 *Read Philippians 1:18-26*

🖊 *Underline* why Paul ***remained faithful*** in verse 25.

📖 *Read Philippians 1:12-14*

🖊 *Underline* the ***reason*** Paul was imprisoned in verse 12.

6. _____

📖 *Read Philippians 1:8*

🖊 *Circle* how Paul ***longed*** for the Philippians.

📖 *Read Galatians 4:19*

    Underline how Paul describes his **wait** for Christ to be formed in the Galatians.

    Read 1 Thessalonians 2:7-8

        Circle the image Paul uses as he describes his **care** for the Thessalonians.

7. _____

    Read 2 Corinthians 11:22-33

        Underline all of Paul's **hardships** found in these verses.

    Read Philippians 3:20-21

        Circle where our **citizenship** is found.

8. _____

    Read Acts 9:22-25

        Underline the Jews **plot** against Paul.

    Read 2 Corinthians 4:7-10

Why would Paul write of all his persecutions and sufferings to the churches of Corinth?

9. _____

    Read Philippians 3:18-19

        Circle the word that describes Paul's **emotional state** as he writes this letter.

How many of these nine things could be taught in a classroom?

NOW WHAT?

Do you have someone to **disciple** you?

The first step in this journey is to identify a **mature** believer that will *invest* in you. You might need to talk with your pastor about helping you to find a discipler.

In the Great Commission, Jesus tells us to teach **everything** that He has commanded. We recommend that you sit down with your discipler, beginning in the book of Matthew, and look at *everything* Jesus taught by His words and His actions.

We have listed two resources that are critical in your growth as a disciple: *Tally Ho the Fox* by Herb Hodges and *Master Plan of Evangelism* by Robert Coleman. We highly recommend that you read these two books to learn about your marching orders of making disciples.

Memorize *Matthew 28:18-20*

PRAYER

Father, thank You for Your example of what it means to make disciples. I pray that this marching order You have given me will become the command that will define my life from this day forward. Please equip me by giving me a disciple that will prepare me to fulfill this order You have given me. I pray that my life will be fruitful and *many* people will look like Jesus because of my faithfulness to Your calling. Use me to reach the nations for Your great name, Lord. Amen.

RECOMMENDED RESOURCES

Book: *Tally Ho the Fox* by Herb Hodges

Book: *The Master Plan of Evangelism* by Robert Coleman

Book: *The Training of the Twelve* by A. B. Bruce

DVD: *Faith Lessons, Volume 6: In the Dust of the Rabbi* by Ray Vander Laan

CONGRATULATIONS!!!

You have completed the first nine footsteps and are ready to continue your life long walk with the Lord Jesus Christ.

THINGS TO REMEMBER
- Meet regularly with a mature believer so they can "rub off on you "and help you continue to grow in the Lord.
- Have a quiet time in prayer and Bible study with the Lord every day.
- Serve Him as He leads.
- Be a good manager of your possessions.
- Share Christ with others and share what you learn with others.
- Become a Disciple Maker.

GLOSSARY

Atoning Sacrifice
See propitiation.

Believe
The word for believe is *pisteúō* which means to be persuaded and have confidence. There is action to belief. Faith is hearing God's voice and belief is putting that into action.

Bond-servant
A bond-servant is someone who belongs to another; a bond-slave is without any ownership rights of their own. This word is used is used with the highest dignity in the NT of believers who willingly live under Christ's authority as His devoted followers. (Discovery Bible)

Church
Church is the total body of believers whom God calls out from the world and into His eternal kingdom. Church is not a building or a place to go. (Discovery Bible)

Confess
Confess is to agree with God that we have sinned. (Discovery Bible)

Covenant
A covenant is a binding agreement between parties. God offers a binding agreement all by calling everyone to enter in a personal, saving relationship with Himself. (Discovery Bible)

Disciple
Disciples are both the people who please the Lord and the people who will reach the world. A disciple is a committed, lifelong learner and follower of Jesus Christ. I must first be a disciple before I can obey His command to make disciples. A disciple is a person who doesn't just want to know what his teacher knows; he wants to be what his teacher is. (Tally Ho the Fox)

Discipler
A discipler, or disciple-maker, is a person who "turns men into disciples." A discipler is a maturing disciple who understands the marching orders of Jesus. A discipler is not a "super Christian" who knows every answer. Rather, a discipler is a co-learner with his disciple who learns and grows together with his disciple. By definition, a discipler must have a disciple. (Tally Ho the Fox)

Disciple-Making

Disciple-making, or discipling, is the process of building men and women into disciples. Disciple-making is simply taking everything God has placed in you and investing it directly into someone else, under the direction of the Holy Spirit. Disciple-making is done by someone, not by something. It is done by persons, not by programs. It is accomplished by individuals, not by institutions. Technically, discipling is one Christian person imparting his whole life to another, by example, leadership, and relationship. Disciple-making is more than a class. It is life transference. (Tally Ho the Fox)

Disciplines

Disciplines are the areas of life that reveal the cost of discipleship. Among others, disciplines include studying your Bible, praying, memorizing Scripture, fellowshipping with other believers, fasting, and being a good steward of His resources. (Tally Ho the Fox)

Faith

Faith is the Lord's inborn persuasion and is always received by believers; it is never self-generated. It is not is not human belief; it is always imparted by the Lord. It is the gift of God from the moment of conversion, to the end of sanctification. (Discovery Bible)

Fellowship

Fellowship means mutually sharing God's gift of salvation and all that it brings to the community of Christians because they are in Christ. Believers are fellow-partners in the true knowledge of God because each belongs to the Lord. Accordingly, they share unique companionship with each other – a kindred spirit (Spirit) and closeness that transcends all racial and economic barriers. (Discovery Bible)

Justification

To make righteous and be divinely-approved. It refers to the Lord changing the status of a believer from condemned to pardoned (from "death to life"). This happens at conversion as believers are released from the penalty of their sin, with an ongoing opportunity to grow in divine approval as sanctification increases as believers are increasingly released from the power of sin. (Discovery Bible)

Propitiation

Propitiation is an offering to appease an offended party. Our sin has offended God. Since all people have broken God's holy Law, all have divine wrath upon them and need redemption. Propitiation is God's answer to everyone's problem of unforgiven sin. Through Christ's blood, the penalty (divine wrath) for our sins was completely satisfied. Jesus sacrificed Himself at Calvary and reconciled repentant offenders with an offended God. By giving His own life, Christ could bring righteousness to forgiven sinners, without comprising God's absolute holiness. Christ's death (shed blood) propitiated all divine judgment on sin. (Discovery Bible)

Reconcile

To decisively change, like when two people change to the same position. When a person becomes a believer and follows Christ, they have changed from condemned to pardoned. (Discovery Bible)

Retribution

Retribution is the full administration of justice and reflects the judge's personal standard. This has obvious implications when the Judge is the Lord – the one possessing absolute holiness and insisting on His eternal purpose. (Discovery Bible)

Reward

Rewards are a future attainment a believer will receive based on their obedience and what they have done for God after they have believed. (Discovery Bible)

Righteousness

Righteousness is the approval of God; His divine approval. Righteousness refers to what is deemed right by the Lord after His examination.. In a believer, this begins with receiving Jesus Christ as Savior and Lord. This changes a person's status before the Lord from condemned to divinely-approved. (Discovery Bible)

Salvation

Salvation is God's gift whereby He rescues believers out of destruction and into His safety. Salvation is a broad term, including all of God's acts of deliverance for believers including freeing them from the penalty and effects of sin. Scripture speaks of salvation in three "phases." (Discovery Bible

- Believers have been saved from the penalty of sin (justification, Ephesians 2:5,8; 2 Timothy 1:9).
- Believers are being saved from the power of sin (sanctification, 1 Corinthians 1:18, 2 Corinthians 2:15, Philippians l 2:12).
- Believers will be saved at Christ's return from the previous effects of sin (glorification, Ro 5:10, 11 Thessalonians 5:8, 22 Thessalonians 2:14)

Sanctification

Sanctification is the process of advancing in holiness. It is used of the believer being progressively transformed by the Lord into His nature. (Discovery Bible)

Sin

Sin is missing the mark and falling short of His mark. Living independent from God and choosing to walk outside His revelation of faith is sin. (Discovery Bible)

Stewardship

Stewardship is utilizing and managing all resources God provides for the glory of God and the betterment of His creation. (Holman Bible Dictionary)
Stewardship is about accountability and responsibility. For the believer, this involves the co-management of God's resources under Him on earth through faith. (Discovery Bible)

Worship

Worship is God revealing Himself or His ways and our responding appropriately to Him.